# EMMANUEL JOSEPH

# Holy Harmony, Balancing Godliness, Work Ambitions, Love, and Ethical

*Copyright © 2025 by Emmanuel Joseph*

*All rights reserved. No part of this publication may be reproduced, stored or transmitted in any form or by any means, electronic, mechanical, photocopying, recording, scanning, or otherwise without written permission from the publisher. It is illegal to copy this book, post it to a website, or distribute it by any other means without permission.*

*First edition*

*This book was professionally typeset on Reedsy. Find out more at reedsy.com*

# Contents

| | | |
|---|---|---|
| 1 | Chapter 1 | 1 |
| 2 | Chapter 1: The Essence of Godliness | 3 |
| 3 | Chapter 2: Defining Work Ambitions | 5 |
| 4 | Chapter 3: Cultivating Love in Relationships | 7 |
| 5 | Chapter 4: Ethical Entrepreneurship Principles | 9 |
| 6 | Chapter 5: Integrating Godliness in the Workplace | 11 |
| 7 | Chapter 6: The Role of Faith in Pursuing Ambitions | 13 |
| 8 | Chapter 7: Harmonizing Love and Career | 15 |
| 9 | Chapter 8: Ethical Entrepreneurship in Action | 16 |
| 10 | Chapter 9: The Power of Purpose-Driven Work | 18 |
| 11 | Chapter 10: Fostering Love in Leadership | 20 |
| 12 | Chapter 11: The Interplay of Godliness and Entrepreneurship | 21 |
| 13 | Chapter 12: Achieving Holy Harmony | 23 |
| 14 | Chapter 13: The Art of Mindfulness | 25 |
| 15 | Chapter 14: The Power of Gratitude | 26 |
| 16 | Chapter 15: The Pursuit of Lifelong Learning | 27 |
| 17 | Chapter 16: Embracing Change with Grace | 29 |
| 18 | Chapter 17: Creating a Legacy of Goodness | 31 |

# 1

# Chapter 1

**Introduction**

In a world that often feels fast-paced and chaotic, finding balance between godliness, work ambitions, love, and ethical entrepreneurship can be a daunting challenge. Yet, it is within this harmonious balance that we discover true fulfillment and purpose. "Holy Harmony: Balancing Godliness, Work Ambitions, Love, and Ethical Entrepreneurship" delves into this intricate dance, offering insights and guidance to achieve a life that resonates with meaning and integrity.

Godliness forms the cornerstone of a balanced life, providing a spiritual foundation that influences our thoughts, actions, and interactions. It is through a deep connection with the divine that we cultivate virtues such as compassion, humility, and righteousness. By prioritizing spiritual growth, we anchor ourselves in values that guide us through the complexities of modern life.

Work ambitions drive us to strive for excellence and make meaningful contributions to our professional fields. However, the pursuit of success can often overshadow other aspects of life if not approached mindfully. This book explores how to align our ambitions with our core values, ensuring that our professional endeavors bring not only personal satisfaction but also positive impacts on society.

Love is the essence of human connections, infusing our relationships with warmth and trust. Cultivating love in our lives requires effort and intentionality, as we seek to build strong and supportive bonds with those around us. By nurturing love, we create a network of emotional support that sustains us through life's trials and triumphs.

Ethical entrepreneurship emerges as a powerful force in the modern world, where businesses have the potential to drive positive change. By conducting business with integrity, transparency, and a commitment to social responsibility, we can create enterprises that benefit not only ourselves but also our communities. This book delves into the principles of ethical entrepreneurship, offering a roadmap for building businesses that reflect our highest ideals.

The journey to achieving holy harmony is not a linear path but a dynamic process that requires ongoing reflection and adjustment. By integrating godliness, work ambitions, love, and ethical entrepreneurship, we can create a life that is balanced, fulfilling, and aligned with our true selves. This book provides practical strategies and inspirational stories to guide readers on this transformative journey.

Ultimately, "Holy Harmony: Balancing Godliness, Work Ambitions, Love, and Ethical Entrepreneurship" is an invitation to embark on a journey of self-discovery and growth. It challenges us to examine our priorities, make intentional choices, and embrace a holistic approach to life. Through this exploration, we can uncover the profound sense of peace and purpose that comes from living in harmony with our values and aspirations.

# 2

# Chapter 1: The Essence of Godliness

Godliness, as an anchor in our lives, serves as the foundation upon which we build our principles, decisions, and actions. It is the embodiment of living a life that reflects divine virtues such as love, compassion, and righteousness. By cultivating a godly character, individuals find a sense of purpose and direction, allowing them to navigate the complexities of life with clarity and conviction.

Moreover, godliness isn't merely about religious observance; it is an active, dynamic expression of faith that influences every aspect of our lives. It calls for an intimate relationship with the divine, characterized by prayer, meditation, and the study of sacred texts. This relationship fosters spiritual growth, nurturing the soul and transforming the individual's outlook on life and their interactions with others.

In a world driven by material pursuits and transient pleasures, maintaining godliness requires conscious effort and discipline. It involves prioritizing spiritual growth over worldly achievements, seeking eternal treasures over temporal gains. This perspective shift enables individuals to live in alignment with their values, finding contentment and peace amid life's challenges.

Ultimately, godliness provides a moral compass, guiding individuals to make ethical choices and act with integrity. It instills a deep sense of accountability to a higher power, fostering a life of honesty, humility, and service to others. By embracing godliness, one cultivates a life that is not only fulfilling but also leaves a lasting positive impact on the world.

# 3

# Chapter 2: Defining Work Ambitions

Work ambitions are the driving force behind our professional endeavors, propelling us toward personal and career growth. These ambitions stem from a desire to achieve excellence, make meaningful contributions, and realize our full potential. They inspire us to set goals, overcome obstacles, and continually strive for improvement.

However, work ambitions must be carefully balanced to avoid becoming all-consuming. While the pursuit of success is commendable, it is essential to maintain a holistic approach that considers physical, emotional, and spiritual well-being. This balance ensures that work remains a source of fulfillment rather than a cause of burnout and stress.

Aligning work ambitions with personal values and purpose is crucial for long-term satisfaction. When our professional goals resonate with our core beliefs and passions, work becomes more than just a means to an end; it transforms into a vocation that brings joy and meaning. This alignment fosters a sense of authenticity and coherence in our lives, promoting overall well-being.

Moreover, work ambitions should be pursued with a spirit of ethical entrepreneurship. This involves conducting business with integrity, fairness, and a commitment to social responsibility. By prioritizing ethical considerations, individuals can achieve success while making a positive impact on society. This approach not only enhances professional reputation but also contributes to a more just and equitable world.

# 4

# Chapter 3: Cultivating Love in Relationships

Love is the cornerstone of human connections, infusing our relationships with warmth, trust, and mutual respect. It is an enduring bond that transcends time and distance, providing emotional support and companionship through life's ups and downs. Cultivating love in relationships requires effort, patience, and a willingness to prioritize the well-being of others.

Communication is a vital component of loving relationships. Open, honest, and empathetic dialogue fosters understanding and deepens emotional intimacy. By actively listening and expressing our thoughts and feelings, we create a safe space where both partners feel valued and heard. This foundation of trust and transparency is essential for maintaining healthy, fulfilling relationships.

Moreover, love thrives on acts of kindness and generosity. Small gestures of appreciation, support, and affection nurture the emotional connection and strengthen the bond between individuals. These acts demonstrate care and commitment, reinforcing the sense of partnership and solidarity in the relationship.

Balancing love with other aspects of life, such as work and personal goals, is essential for sustaining healthy relationships. This balance involves setting boundaries, managing time effectively, and prioritizing moments of togetherness. By ensuring that love remains a central focus, individuals can build lasting, meaningful connections that enrich their lives and foster personal growth.

# 5

# Chapter 4: Ethical Entrepreneurship Principles

Ethical entrepreneurship is the practice of conducting business with integrity, transparency, and a commitment to social responsibility. It involves creating value not only for shareholders but also for employees, customers, and the broader community. This approach prioritizes ethical considerations, ensuring that business practices align with moral values and contribute to the common good.

Central to ethical entrepreneurship is the principle of fairness. This involves treating all stakeholders with respect and equity, ensuring that business decisions are made with consideration of their impact on others. Fairness extends to employee relations, customer interactions, and partnerships, fostering a culture of trust and mutual benefit.

Sustainability is another key aspect of ethical entrepreneurship. This involves adopting practices that minimize environmental impact and promote long-term ecological health. By prioritizing sustainability, businesses can contribute to the preservation of natural resources and the well-being of future generations. This approach not only enhances corporate reputation but also fosters a sense of corporate citizenship.

Moreover, ethical entrepreneurship emphasizes social responsibility. This involves contributing to the welfare of the community through charitable initiatives, fair labor practices, and inclusive policies. By addressing social issues and supporting underserved populations, businesses can make a meaningful difference in society. This commitment to social responsibility enhances brand loyalty and creates a positive legacy.

# 6

# Chapter 5: Integrating Godliness in the Workplace

Bringing godliness into the workplace involves embodying spiritual values in professional interactions and decisions. This integration fosters a culture of integrity, compassion, and ethical behavior, creating a positive and supportive work environment. By prioritizing godliness, individuals can navigate workplace challenges with grace and wisdom.

One way to integrate godliness is through servant leadership. This approach emphasizes leading by example, prioritizing the needs of others, and fostering a culture of collaboration and mutual respect. Servant leaders inspire trust and loyalty, creating a work environment where employees feel valued and motivated to contribute their best efforts.

Moreover, incorporating godliness in the workplace involves practicing empathy and compassion. This means understanding and addressing the needs and concerns of colleagues, customers, and stakeholders. By showing genuine care and consideration, individuals can build strong relationships and create a supportive, inclusive work culture.

Ethical decision-making is another crucial aspect of integrating godliness. This involves making choices that align with moral values and consider the broader impact on society. By prioritizing ethical considerations, individuals can navigate complex business decisions with integrity and uphold a reputation of trustworthiness and accountability.

7

# Chapter 6: The Role of Faith in Pursuing Ambitions

Faith serves as a guiding light in the pursuit of work ambitions, providing strength, resilience, and a sense of purpose. It offers a foundation of unwavering trust in divine guidance, enabling individuals to navigate challenges and uncertainties with confidence. By grounding their ambitions in faith, individuals can find meaning and fulfillment in their professional endeavors.

Faith instills a sense of perseverance, encouraging individuals to remain steadfast in the face of obstacles. It provides the assurance that challenges are opportunities for growth and that success is achievable with determination and dedication. This perspective fosters a positive mindset, enabling individuals to overcome setbacks and continue striving toward their goals.

Moreover, faith encourages humility and gratitude. It reminds individuals to acknowledge their blessings and recognize the contributions of others in their journey. By maintaining a posture of gratitude, individuals can build stronger relationships and create a positive work environment that fosters collaboration and mutual support.

Faith also promotes ethical behavior in the pursuit of ambitions. It calls for individuals to act with integrity, fairness, and respect for others. By aligning their actions with their spiritual values, individuals can achieve success while upholding moral principles and contributing to the common good.

# 8

# Chapter 7: Harmonizing Love and Career

Balancing love and career involves prioritizing both personal relationships and professional goals in a way that fosters harmony and fulfillment. This balance requires effective time management, clear communication, and a commitment to nurturing both aspects of life. By finding harmony between love and career, individuals can lead a more balanced and satisfying life.

Effective time management is crucial for harmonizing love and career. This involves setting boundaries and allocating dedicated time for both work and personal relationships. By being intentional with their time, individuals can ensure that they are fully present in both areas and avoid neglecting their loved ones or professional responsibilities.

Clear communication is another essential component of this balance. Open and honest dialogue about expectations, needs, and priorities helps to create mutual understanding and support. By actively listening and expressing their thoughts and feelings, individuals can strengthen their relationships and navigate the demands of work and love more effectively.

Moreover, nurturing both love and career involves making intentional choices that align with personal values and goals. This means seeking opportunities for growth and fulfillment in both areas and being willing to make adjustments as needed. By prioritizing what truly matters, individuals can create a sense of harmony and contentment in their lives.

# 9

# Chapter 8: Ethical Entrepreneurship in Action

Putting ethical entrepreneurship into practice involves adopting strategies and principles that promote integrity, sustainability, and social responsibility. This approach requires a commitment to ethical decision-making and a focus on creating value for all stakeholders. By implementing ethical practices, businesses can achieve long-term success while contributing positively to society.

One key strategy for ethical entrepreneurship is adopting transparent and accountable business practices. This involves clear communication, honest reporting, and adherence to regulatory standards. Transparency builds trust with stakeholders and fosters a culture of integrity, enhancing the business's reputation and credibility.

Sustainability is also a critical component of ethical entrepreneurship. This means adopting environmentally friendly practices, such as reducing waste, conserving resources, and promoting renewable energy. By prioritizing sustainability, businesses can minimize their environmental impact and contribute to a healthier planet.

Social responsibility is another essential aspect of ethical entrepreneurship. This involves supporting community initiatives, implementing fair labor practices, and promoting diversity and inclusion. By addressing social issues and creating opportunities for underserved populations, businesses can make a meaningful impact on society and build strong community relations.

# 10

# Chapter 9: The Power of Purpose-Driven Work

Purpose-driven work is the pursuit of professional endeavors that align with one's values and passions, creating a sense of meaning and fulfillment. This approach involves seeking opportunities that resonate with personal beliefs and contribute to a greater good. By embracing purpose-driven work, individuals can experience a profound sense of satisfaction and motivation in their careers.

Aligning work with purpose requires introspection and clarity about one's values and goals. This involves identifying the core principles that guide decisions and actions, as well as the passions that ignite enthusiasm and drive. By understanding what truly matters, individuals can make informed career choices that reflect their authentic selves.

Purpose-driven work also fosters a sense of commitment and dedication. When individuals feel that their work contributes to a larger cause, they are more likely to persevere through challenges and maintain a positive attitude. This sense of purpose fuels resilience and inspires a consistent effort to achieve excellence.

Moreover, purpose-driven work promotes ethical behavior and social responsibility. It calls for individuals to act with integrity and consider the impact of their actions on others. By prioritizing ethical considerations, individuals can contribute to a positive work environment and make meaningful contributions to society. This approach not only enhances personal fulfillment but also creates a legacy of positive change.

# 11

## Chapter 10: Fostering Love in Leadership

Love in leadership is the practice of leading with compassion, empathy, and a genuine concern for the well-being of others. This approach creates a supportive and inclusive work culture, where employees feel valued and motivated to contribute their best efforts. By fostering love in leadership, individuals can inspire trust, loyalty, and collaboration.

Leading with love involves practicing active listening and showing genuine interest in the needs and concerns of team members. This creates an environment where individuals feel heard and understood, fostering a sense of belonging and psychological safety. By prioritizing open communication and empathy, leaders can build strong, cohesive teams.

Compassionate leadership also involves providing support and encouragement to help team members grow and succeed. This means recognizing individual strengths and providing opportunities for development and advancement. By investing in the personal and professional growth of employees, leaders can cultivate a motivated and high-performing team.

Moreover, leading with love requires a commitment to fairness and equity. This involves treating all team members with respect and ensuring that decisions are made with consideration of their impact on others. By promoting a culture of inclusivity and fairness, leaders can create a positive work environment that fosters collaboration and mutual respect.

# 12

## Chapter 11: The Interplay of Godliness and Entrepreneurship

The interplay of godliness and entrepreneurship involves integrating spiritual values into business practices to create a harmonious and ethical approach to entrepreneurship. This integration fosters a sense of purpose and integrity, guiding individuals to make decisions that align with their moral principles and contribute to the common good.

Godliness in entrepreneurship calls for a commitment to ethical behavior and social responsibility. This means conducting business with honesty, transparency, and fairness, ensuring that all stakeholders are treated with respect and consideration. By prioritizing ethical considerations, entrepreneurs can build a reputation of trustworthiness and integrity.

Moreover, godliness promotes a sense of accountability to a higher power, encouraging individuals to act with humility and gratitude. This perspective fosters a commitment to giving back to the community and making a positive impact on society. By embracing godliness, entrepreneurs can create businesses that are not only successful but also contribute to the greater good.

The integration of godliness and entrepreneurship also involves seeking divine guidance in decision-making. This means relying on prayer, meditation, and spiritual discernment to navigate business challenges and opportunities. By trusting in a higher power, entrepreneurs can find clarity and confidence in their choices, leading to a more fulfilling and purpose-driven approach to business.

# 13

# Chapter 12: Achieving Holy Harmony

Achieving holy harmony involves balancing godliness, work ambitions, love, and ethical entrepreneurship to create a fulfilling and meaningful life. This balance requires intentional effort, self-reflection, and a commitment to aligning actions with values. By pursuing holy harmony, individuals can experience a sense of peace, purpose, and fulfillment in all aspects of life.

The first step in achieving holy harmony is cultivating a strong foundation of godliness. This involves nurturing a relationship with the divine and prioritizing spiritual growth. By grounding their lives in faith, individuals can find direction and clarity in their pursuits, ensuring that their actions reflect their values.

Balancing work ambitions with personal values and ethical considerations is also crucial for achieving holy harmony. This means pursuing professional goals with integrity and a commitment to social responsibility. By aligning work with purpose and ethical principles, individuals can achieve success while making a positive impact on society.

Moreover, nurturing loving relationships is essential for a fulfilling life. This involves prioritizing meaningful connections and practicing empathy, kindness, and communication. By fostering love in personal and professional relationships, individuals can create a supportive and enriching environment that enhances their well-being.

Ultimately, achieving holy harmony is an ongoing journey that requires mindfulness, intention, and a willingness to make adjustments as needed. By striving for balance in all aspects of life, individuals can create a sense of harmony and fulfillment that resonates with their true selves and contributes to the greater good.

# 14

# Chapter 13: The Art of Mindfulness

Mindfulness, the practice of being fully present and engaged in the moment, plays a crucial role in achieving holy harmony. By cultivating mindfulness, individuals can develop a deeper awareness of their thoughts, feelings, and actions, leading to greater self-understanding and emotional balance. This practice enhances overall well-being and fosters a sense of inner peace.

Incorporating mindfulness into daily life involves setting aside time for meditation, reflection, and mindful activities. These practices help to quiet the mind, reduce stress, and enhance focus. By regularly engaging in mindfulness, individuals can create a sense of calm and clarity that permeates all aspects of life.

Moreover, mindfulness promotes a more compassionate and empathetic approach to relationships. By being fully present with others, individuals can listen more deeply, understand their perspectives, and respond with greater sensitivity. This fosters stronger connections and enhances the quality of interactions, contributing to more fulfilling and harmonious relationships.

Mindfulness also enhances decision-making and problem-solving abilities. By approaching challenges with a calm and focused mind, individuals can gain greater insight and clarity, leading to more effective and thoughtful solutions. This practice empowers individuals to navigate life's complexities with confidence and grace.

# 15

# Chapter 14: The Power of Gratitude

Gratitude is a powerful practice that can transform one's outlook on life and foster a sense of contentment and joy. By regularly expressing gratitude for the blessings and opportunities in life, individuals can cultivate a positive mindset and enhance their overall well-being. This practice helps to shift focus from what is lacking to what is abundant and fulfilling.

Incorporating gratitude into daily life involves making a conscious effort to acknowledge and appreciate the positive aspects of one's experiences. This can be done through journaling, verbal expressions of thanks, or simple moments of reflection. By consistently practicing gratitude, individuals can create a habit of looking for the good in every situation.

Gratitude also strengthens relationships by fostering a sense of appreciation and acknowledgment. Expressing gratitude to loved ones, colleagues, and even strangers can create a positive ripple effect, enhancing the quality of interactions and building stronger connections. This practice encourages a culture of kindness and mutual respect.

Moreover, gratitude promotes resilience and a positive attitude in the face of challenges. By focusing on the aspects of life that bring joy and fulfillment, individuals can maintain a sense of hope and optimism, even during difficult times. This perspective fosters inner strength and empowers individuals to navigate adversity with grace and determination.

# 16

# Chapter 15: The Pursuit of Lifelong Learning

Lifelong learning is the continuous pursuit of knowledge and personal growth, essential for adapting to the ever-changing world and achieving holy harmony. This practice involves seeking opportunities for education and self-improvement, both formally and informally. By embracing lifelong learning, individuals can remain curious, open-minded, and resilient.

Engaging in lifelong learning involves exploring a variety of subjects and interests. This can include taking courses, reading books, attending workshops, and engaging in meaningful conversations. By continually expanding one's knowledge and skills, individuals can stay intellectually stimulated and adaptable to new challenges and opportunities.

Moreover, lifelong learning fosters a growth mindset, the belief that abilities and intelligence can be developed through dedication and effort. This mindset encourages individuals to embrace challenges, learn from mistakes, and persist in the face of setbacks. By cultivating a growth mindset, individuals can achieve greater personal and professional success.

Lifelong learning also enhances creativity and innovation. By exposing oneself to new ideas and perspectives, individuals can develop a more diverse and enriched understanding of the world. This fosters creative thinking and the ability to approach problems from multiple angles, leading to more innovative solutions and a more fulfilling life.

17

# Chapter 16: Embracing Change with Grace

Change is an inevitable part of life, and embracing it with grace is essential for achieving holy harmony. By developing a positive and adaptive attitude towards change, individuals can navigate life's transitions with resilience and optimism. This approach fosters personal growth and enhances overall well-being.

Embracing change involves recognizing that change is a natural and necessary aspect of growth. It requires letting go of the fear of the unknown and embracing the possibilities that change can bring. By shifting perspective and viewing change as an opportunity for growth and renewal, individuals can approach transitions with a sense of excitement and curiosity.

Moreover, developing resilience is crucial for navigating change effectively. This involves building emotional strength, practicing self-care, and seeking support from loved ones. By nurturing resilience, individuals can maintain a sense of stability and confidence, even during times of uncertainty and upheaval.

Embracing change also involves being open to new experiences and learning from them. This means staying curious, adaptable, and willing to step outside of one's comfort zone. By embracing new opportunities and challenges, individuals can expand their horizons, develop new skills, and enrich their lives.

# 18

# Chapter 17: Creating a Legacy of Goodness

Creating a legacy of goodness involves living a life that positively impacts others and contributes to the betterment of society. This practice requires intentionality, compassion, and a commitment to making a difference. By striving to leave a positive legacy, individuals can create a sense of purpose and fulfillment in their lives.

A key aspect of creating a legacy of goodness is practicing kindness and compassion. This involves treating others with respect, empathy, and generosity. By consistently demonstrating these qualities, individuals can inspire others and create a ripple effect of positivity and goodwill.

Moreover, contributing to the community and supporting charitable initiatives is an essential part of leaving a positive legacy. This can involve volunteering, donating to causes, and advocating for social justice. By actively participating in efforts to improve society, individuals can create lasting change and make a meaningful impact.

Creating a legacy of goodness also involves mentoring and empowering others. By sharing knowledge, skills, and experiences, individuals can help others achieve their goals and reach their full potential. This practice fosters a culture of collaboration and support, contributing to the growth and success of future generations.

Ultimately, living with integrity and aligning actions with values is central to creating a positive legacy. By making ethical choices and acting with honesty and accountability, individuals can build a reputation of trustworthiness and leave a lasting, positive impact on the world.

**Holy Harmony: Balancing Godliness, Work Ambitions, Love, and Ethical Entrepreneurship** is a profound exploration of how to weave the threads of spirituality, ambition, love, and ethics into a tapestry of a balanced, fulfilling life. This book delves deep into the essence of godliness, offering insights on how to cultivate a strong spiritual foundation that anchors our lives amidst the chaos of modernity. It also examines the pursuit of work ambitions, guiding readers to align their professional goals with their core values, ensuring that their careers bring both personal satisfaction and societal benefit.

Love, the cornerstone of human relationships, is thoroughly explored, providing practical advice on nurturing meaningful connections that support and sustain us. Ethical entrepreneurship, a beacon of hope in today's business world, is dissected with principles and practices that promote integrity, social responsibility, and sustainable success. Each chapter offers actionable strategies and inspirational stories that illuminate the path to achieving holy harmony.

This book is an invitation to embark on a transformative journey of self-discovery and growth, challenging readers to examine their priorities and embrace a holistic approach to life. Through the integration of godliness, work ambitions, love, and ethical entrepreneurship, **Holy Harmony** reveals the profound sense of peace and purpose that comes from living in alignment with one's true values and aspirations. It is a guide for those seeking to create a life that is not only balanced but also deeply fulfilling and impactful.

www.ingramcontent.com/pod-product-compliance
Lightning Source LLC
LaVergne TN
LVHW010442070526
838199LV00066B/6151